CW00346274

the **Staffordshire** Bull Terrier

A guide to selection, care, nutrition,
behaviour, breeding and health

about pets

Content

the **Staffordshire Bull Terrier**

Foreword

The book you are holding right now is by no means a complete book about the Staffordshire Bull Terrier. If we had collected all the information about the breed, its history and development, feeding, training, health, and whatever else there is to know, this book would have consisted of at least three hundred pages.

What we have done, however, is to bring together all the basic information that you as a (future) owner of a Staffordshire Bull Terrier need to know in order to handle your pet responsibly. Unfortunately, there are still people who buy a pet without thinking through what they are about to get into.

This book generally deals with the history of the breed, the breed standard and the advantages and disadvantages of buying a Staffordshire Bull Terrier. It also contains essential information about feeding your dog and about the very first steps in training it. Reproduction, day-to-day care, and health and illnesses are also topics.

After having read this book, you can make a carefully considered decision to buy a Staffordshire Bull Terrier and to keep it as a pet in a responsible manner. We advise you, however, not to rely on this book only. A well-reared and trained dog is more than just a dog. Invest therefore in a puppy training course or an obedience course. There are also plenty of excellent books that deal with certain aspects for which we do not have the space in this small book.

About Pets

A Publication of About Pets.

Copyright © 2003
About Pets
co-publisher United Kingdom
Kingdom Books
PO9 5TL, England

ISBN 1852791977
First printing December 2004
Second printing 2005
Third revised printing 2006

Original title: de Staffordshire bull terrier
© 2004 Welzo Media Productions bv,
About Pets bv,
Warffum, the Netherlands
www.aboutpets.info

Photos:
Rob Dekker, Isabelle Francoise,
Kingdom Books, Fam. Vandermeijden,
Rene Verheul, J. Klijn, I. Steijns and
Ton van Gorp

Printed in China

In past centuries, dogs with heavy heads, short muzzles and strong jaws used to be bred. Such dogs were praised for the same physical and mental characteristics that can be found in the Staffordshire Bull Terrier today.

Origins

The bulldog type originated from Molossers. These dogs were quite similar to today's Great Dane. Ever since prehistoric times, the Molossers were used as war dogs and, at the same time, to guard the storage rooms. These big dogs with their heavy heads, short snouts and strong jaws were known particularly for their fearlessness and their biting power. They were used on the battlefields to jump at the throats of horses and thus cause the enemy to fall.

When, due to changes in warfare techniques, these dogs became superfluous on the battlefields, their new role was to entertain the aristocracy by fighting against bears, bulls and wolves in the arena. The Celts had also bred a similar dog, the Mastiff.
Bull fights became increasingly popular in Great Britain. In this sport, the dog was used to fight against a bull. These dogs became known under the name of 'bulldog' or 'bull baiter', words originating from 'bull baiting', the original name of this sport.

When the English aristocracy lost its interest in bull baiting, it became a favourite pastime with the common people. The big dogs

to breed smaller, more mobile dogs. The bulls, which now had a clear advantage, were tied up in fights from now on.

At around 1830, dog fights gained popularity in England. The bulldogs of the time, with their short snouts and undershot jaws, were ideally built to grip the bull at its nose and to hold on for as long as necessary. This fighting technique was not as popular in dog fights (it was not spectacular enough). The search was on for dogs with longer muzzles, which grabbed their opponents again and again. Their teeth had to be bigger and their jaws had to close correctly to ensure a good bite. Shorter legs were also an advantage, as a dog with a low-lying centre of gravity is less easily knocked over. These dogs were called 'bulldog terriers'. The winner of a dog fight was the dog that refused to 'surrender'. The winning dog was thus not necessarily the best fighter. Even today, the most valued characteristics of the Staffordshire Bull Terrier are its fearlessness and its determination.

All animal fighting was prohibited later in the nineteenth century. The Staffordshire Bull Terrier thus had to survive almost a century as just a pet. The breeding focussed on preserving the breed-specific characteristics, whereby the breed was made more sociable so that it was more suited to its duties as a pet.

The English breed association was founded in Cradley Heath, Staffordshire, in 1935. This is how the dog got the name Staffordshire Bull Terrier.

UK Kennel Club and their breed standards

What does the UK Kennel Club? To say it in their own words: "The Kennel Club is committed to developing and supporting a nation of responsible dog owners. As well as organising events and campaigns to help dog owners meet their responsibilities, the Kennel Club also produces a range of literature to assist the dog owning public."

What is the use of a Breed Standard? The Kennel clubs answer: "The basis of breed shows is the judging of dogs

against the 'Breed Standard', which is the prescribed blueprint of the particular breed of dog. For all licensed breed shows, the Kennel Club Breed Standards must be used for the judging of dogs."

More about the UK Kennel Club Breed Standards: "The Breed Standards are owned by the Kennel Club, and all changes are subject to approval by the Kennel Club General Committee. New Breed Standards, for newly recognised breeds, are drawn up once the breed has become sufficiently established within the UK. Careful research is conducted into the historical background, health and temperament of any new breed before Kennel Club recognition is granted. The Kennel Club currently recognises 196 breeds. Upon recognition, breeds are placed on the Imported Breed Register until they are deemed eligible for transferral to the Breed Register".

A standard provides a guideline for breeders and judges. It is something of an ideal that dogs of each breed must strive to match. With some breeds, dogs are already being bred that match the ideal. Other breeds have a long way to go. There is a list of defects for each breed. These can be serious defects that disqualify the dog, in which case it will be excluded from breeding. Permitted defects are not serious, but do cost points in a show.

The UK Kennel Club breed standard for the Staffordshire Bull Terrier

General Appearance
Smooth-coated, well balanced, of great strength for his size. Muscular, active and agile.

Characteristics
Traditionally of indomitable courage and tenacity. Highly intelligent and affectionate especially with children.

Temperament
Bold, fearless and totally reliable.

Head and Skull
Short, deep though with broad skull. Very pronounced cheek muscles, distinct stop, short foreface, nose black.

Eyes
Dark preferred but may bear some relation to coat colour. Round, of medium size, and set to look straight ahead. Eye rims dark.

Ears
Rose or half pricked, not large or heavy. Full, drop or pricked ears highly undesirable.

Mouth
Lips tight and clean. Jaws strong, teeth large, with a perfect, regular and complete scissor bite, i.e. upper teeth closely overlapping lower teeth and set square to the jaws.

Neck
Muscular, rather short, clean in outline gradually widening towards shoulders.

Forequarters
Legs straight and well boned, set rather wide apart, showing no weakness at the pasterns, from which point feet turn out a little. Shoulders well laid back with no looseness at elbow.

Body
Close-coupled, with level topline, wide front, deep brisket, well sprung ribs; muscular and well defined.

Hindquarters
Well muscled, hocks well let down with stifles well bent. Legs parallel when viewed from behind.

Feet
Well padded, strong and of medium size. Nails black in solid coloured dogs.

Tail
Medium length, low-set, tapering to a point and carried rather low. Should not curl much and may be likened to an old-fashioned pump handle.

Gait/Movement
Free, powerful and agile with economy of effort. Legs moving parallel when viewed from front or rear. Discernible drive from hindlegs.

Coat
Smooth, short and close. Colour Red, fawn, white, black or blue, or any one of these colours with white. Any shade of brindle or any shade of brindle with white. Black and tan or liver colour highly undesirable.

Size
Desirable height at withers 36-41 cms (14 to 16 ins), these heights being related to the weights. Weight: dogs: 13-17 kgs (28-38 lb); bitches 11-15.4 kgs.

Faults
Any departure from the foregoing points should be considered a fault and the seriousness with which the fault should be regarded should be in exact proportion to its degree and its effect upon the health and welfare of the dog.

Note
Male animals should have two apparently normal testicles fully descended into the scrotum.
September 2000

Breed standard by courtesy of the Kennel Club of Great Britain.

Once you have made that properly considered decision to buy a dog, you have various options. Do you want a puppy, an adult dog, or even an older dog? Would you rather have a bitch or a dog?

When choosing a Stafford, it is advisable to buy a pedigree dog. Of course, the question also arises as to where to get your dog; from a private person, a reliable breeder, or from an animal shelter? It is important for you and the animal that you sort out all theses things in advance, as you want to make sure that you get a dog that suits your circumstances. With a puppy, you choose a playful, energetic housemate that finds it easy to adapt to its new environment. If you prefer things a bit quieter, an older dog is a good choice. Contact the breed association about the possibilities of buying an adult dog.

Advantages and disadvantages

The Staffordshire Bull Terrier has been bred as a companion dog for many generations. It is therefore a friendly dog, oriented towards human company. The Stafford is very sociable and not at all shy. It will not wait for visitors to caress it, and will happily introduce itself. It is a dog of medium size and thus fits into almost any home quite well. The Stafford's coat is smooth and short and needs little care. The Staffordshire Bull Terrier is a sporty dog, which really enjoys going for walks or running next to the bike, and it possesses great stamina (when trained).

One of the disadvantages of the Staffordshire Bull Terrier is that it is a bad guard dog. If you are looking for a dog to protect house and hearth, you need to look at other breeds. Most Staffords also dislike water. If you are a fan of water sports, you might be better off choosing a gundog breed. Another very important point to bear in mind is that a Stafford will never miss a fight. It will not attack of its own accord, but should your Stafford get involved in a fight, there can quite easily be some serious casualties. Take this into consideration when thinking about buying a Staffordshire Bull Terrier. In many European countries, Staffordshire Bull Terriers are classed as dangerous dogs and are thus subject to certain laws and restrictions. This does not apply to the UK, however. Here they are actually one of the most commonly found breeds.

Male or female?

Whether you choose a male or a female puppy, or an adult dog or bitch, is an entirely personal decision. A male typically needs more leadership because he tends to be more dominant by nature. He will try to play boss over other dogs and, if he gets the chance, over people too. In the wild, the most dominant dog (or wolf) is always the leader of the pack. In many cases this is a male. A bitch is usually much more focussed on her master, as she sees him as the pack leader.

A puppy test is good for defining what kind of character a young dog will develop. During a test one usually sees that a dog is more dominant than a bitch. You can often quickly recognise the bossy, the adventurous and the cautious characters. So visit the litter a couple of times early on. Try to pick a puppy that suits your own personality. Explain to the breeder what type of dog you are looking for and what your plans are with the animal. Are you looking for a puppy with which you will be able to go to shows later, or would you prefer to do dog sports? Ask the breeder for advice, as he knows his puppies best. A dominant dog, for instance, needs a strong hand. It will often try to see how far it can go. You must regularly make it clear who's the boss, and that it must obey all the members of the family.

Puppy ...

... or adult?

When bitches are sexually mature, they will go into season. On average, a bitch is in season twice a year for about two to three weeks. This is the fertile period when she can mate. Particularly in the second half of her season, she will want to go looking for a dog to mate with. A dog will show more masculine traits once he is sexually mature. He will make sure other dogs know what territory is his by urinating as often as possible in as many places as he can. He will also be difficult to restrain if there's a bitch in season nearby. As far as normal care is concerned, there is little difference between a dog and a bitch.

Puppy or adult?

After you've decided on a male or a female, the next question comes up. Should it be a puppy or an adult dog? Your household circumstances usually play a major role here. Of course, it's great having a sweet little puppy in the house, but bringing up a young dog takes a lot of time. In its first year it learns more than during the rest of its life. This is the period when the foundations are laid for elementary matters, such as house-training, obedience and social behaviour.

You must reckon with the fact that your puppy will keep you busy for a couple of hours a day, certainly in the first few months. You won't need so much time with a grown dog. It has already been brought up, but this doesn't mean it doesn't need correcting from time to time.

A puppy will no doubt leave a trail of destruction in its wake for the first few months. With a little bad

luck, this will cost you some rolls of wallpaper, some good shoes and a few socks. In the worst case you'll be left with some chewed furniture. Some puppies even manage to tear curtains from their rails. With good upbringing this 'vandalism' will quickly disappear, but you won't have to worry about this if you get an older dog. However small a Staffordshire Bull Terrier puppy might be, it will manage to dismantle anything it can reach. It is therefore advisable to buy an indoor kennel for your puppy.

The greatest advantage of buying a puppy, of course, is that you can bring it up your own way. And the upbringing a dog gets (or doesn't get) is a major influence on its whole character. Finally, financial aspects may play a role in your decision. A puppy is generally (much) more expensive than an adult dog, not only in purchase price but also in 'maintenance'. A puppy needs to go to the vet's more often for the necessary vaccinations and check-ups.

Overall, bringing up a puppy requires a good deal of energy, time and money, but you have its upbringing in your own hands. An adult dog costs less money and time, but its character has already been formed. You should also try to find out about the background of an adult dog. Its previous owner may have formed its character in somewhat less positive ways.

Two dogs?

Having two or more dogs in the house is not just nice for us, but also for the animals themselves. Dogs get a lot of pleasure from company of their own kind. After all, they are pack animals. Although Staffordshire Bull Terriers are very focused on their master and family, they still enjoy more company and being with other dogs.

Staffordshire Bull Terriers can be kept together quite easily. If you're sure that you want two young dogs, it's best not to buy them at the same time. Bringing a dog up and establishing the bond between dog and master takes time, and you need to give a lot of attention to your dog in this phase. Having two puppies in the house means you have to divide your attention between them. Apart from that, there's a danger that they will focus on one another rather than on their master. Make sure that the age difference between the two dogs is

approximately two years. This is because the Stafford matures quite late mentally (when it is approximately two years).

It is absolutely not a good idea to buy two male Staffordshire Bull Terriers. Two dogs might get along quite well for some time, but if they do start a fight at one point, they will probably never get along again afterwards.

Bitches can be kept together quite easily, but you do need to be aware of their character. Never put two dominant bitches together, as you can almost guarantee that this couple will start a fight. Bitches do fight once in a while, but they can normally be left together again after a short time. In practice, there are a lot of breeders who keep several bitches together.

An even better combination is a dog and a bitch, as dogs are quite happy to endure bitches with an attitude. You do need to bear in mind, of course, that the bitch will come on heat, and that you need to keep the bitch and the dog separated during this time if you want to avoid having puppies.

It is advisable to keep two Staffords apart at night, and also not to leave them in a room together without supervision. Do not take any risks, and stick to having only one dog if you cannot keep them apart.

A dog and children

Dogs and children are a great combination. They can play together and get great pleasure out of each other's company. Moreover, children need to learn how to handle living beings; they develop respect and a sense of responsibility by caring for a dog (or another pet).

However sweet a dog is, children must understand that it is an animal and not a toy. A dog isn't comfortable when it's being messed around with. It can become frightened, nervous and even aggressive as a result. So make it clear what a dog likes and what it doesn't. Look for ways the child can play with the dog, perhaps a game of hide-and-seek where the child hides and the dog has to find it. Even a simple tennis ball can provide enormous pleasure. Children must learn to leave a dog in peace when it doesn't want to play any more. The dog must therefore have its own place where it's not disturbed. Let your children help with your dog's care as much as possible. A strong bond will be the result.

The arrival of a baby also means changes in the life of a dog. Before the birth you can help get the dog acquainted with the new situation. Let it sniff at the new things in the house and it will quickly accept them. When the baby has arrived, involve the dog in day-by-day events as much as possible, but make sure it gets plenty of attention too.

Never leave a dog alone with young children! Crawling infants sometimes make unexpected movements, which can easily frighten a dog. Infants are also hugely curious, and may try to find out whether the tail is really fastened to the dog, or whether its eyes come out, just like they do with their cuddly toys. But a dog is a dog and it will defend itself when it feels threatened.

Where to buy

There are various ways of acquiring a dog. The decision for

out for breed-specific illnesses and in-breeding. The puppies are taken away from the mother as quickly as possible and are thus insufficiently socialised. Never buy a puppy which is too young and of which you did not get to see the mother and/or the papers.

Luckily, there are plenty of bona-fide breeders of Staffordshire Bull Terriers in the UK. Try to visit several breeders before buying a puppy. Also find out if the breeder is willing to help you after you have bought the puppy and to help you look for solutions if problems should arise.

Finally, you must realise that a pedigree is nothing more or less than a proof of descent. The Kennel Club also issues pedigrees to the young of parents that suffer from congenital conditions, or that have never been checked for them. A pedigree says nothing about the health of the parent dogs.

If you would rather buy an adult dog, you can contact the breed association. They sometimes help with re-homing adult dogs that can no longer be kept by their owners due to circumstances (such as impulse buying, moving home, divorce or work-related matters).

a puppy or an adult dog will also determine to a great extent where you buy your dog.

If it is to be a puppy, you need to find a reliable breeder with a litter. If you choose a popular breed such as the Staffordshire Bull Terrier, you will have plenty of choice. This also means, however, that you will come across dogs that have only been bred for profit's sake. You can see how many puppies are for sale by looking in the classified section of your local newspaper every Saturday. Some of these dogs have pedigrees, but many don't. In so-called 'puppy farms', breeders also often do not look

What to watch out for

Buying a puppy is no simple matter. You must pay attention to the following:

- Never buy a puppy on impulse, even if it is love at first sight. A dog is a living being that will need a lot of care and attention over a period of twelve to fourteen years. It is not a toy that you can put away when you're done with it.
- When re-homing a dog, do not make a decision over night. Ask to take the dog on trial for a few weeks to see if you really get along.
- Take a good look at the mother. Is she calm, nervous, aggressive, well cared for or neglected? The behaviour and condition of the mother is not only a sign of the quality of the breeder, but also of the puppy you're about to buy.

- Avoid buying a puppy whose mother has been kept in a kennel only. A young dog needs as many different impressions as possible during its first few months, including living in a family. It gets used to people and possibly other pets this way. Kennel dogs miss these experiences and are inadequately socialised as a result.
- Always ask to see the parents' papers (vaccination certificates, pedigrees, official health examination reports).
- Never buy a puppy younger than eight weeks.
- Put all agreements with the breeder in writing. A model agreement is available from the breed association.

Travelling with your Staffordshire Bull Terrier

There are a few things to think about before travelling with your dog. While one dog may enjoy travelling, another may hate it.

While you might enjoy going on holidays to far-away places, it is questionable whether your Stafford does, too.

That very first trip

The first trip of a puppy's life is also the most nerve-wrecking. This is the trip from the breeder's to its new home. If possible, pick up your puppy in the morning. It then has the whole day to get used to its new situation. Ask the breeder not to feed the puppy that day. The young animal will be overwhelmed by all kinds of new experiences. Firstly, it's away from its mother; it's in a small room (the car) with all its different smells, noises and strange people. So there's a big chance that the puppy will be carsick this first time, with the annoying consequence that it will remember travelling in the car as an unpleasant experience.

It's thus important to make this first trip as pleasant as possible. When picking up your puppy, always take someone with you who can sit in the back seat with the puppy on his or her lap and talk to it calmly. If it's too warm for the puppy, a place on the floor at the feet of your companion is ideal. The pup will lie there relatively quietly and may even take a nap. Ask the breeder for a cloth or something else that has been lying in the nest and thus has a familiar scent. The puppy can lie on this in the car, and it will also help if it feels lonely during the first nights at home.

If the trip home is a long one, then stop for a break (once in a while). Let your puppy roam and sniff around (on the lead!), offer it a little drink of water and, if necessary, let it do its business. Do take care to lay an old towel in the car. It can happen that the puppy, in its nervousness, may urinate or be sick. It's also good advice to give a puppy positive experiences with car journeys as soon as possible. Make short trips to nice places where you can walk and play with it. It can be a real nuisance if your dog doesn't like travelling in a car. There will always be times when you need to take your dog somewhere in the car, for example to the vet's or to visit family and friends.

Taking your Staffordshire Bull Terrier on holidays

When making holiday plans, you also need to think about what you're going to do with your dog during that time. Are you taking it with you, putting it into kennels or leaving it with friends? In any event there are a number of things you need to do in good time.

If you want to take your dog with you, you need to be sure in advance that it will be welcome at your holiday destination, and what

the rules there are. As mentioned earlier, some countries class Staffords as dangerous dogs and thus subject them to special rules. Therefore check if any such rules apply at your travel destination if you intend to go abroad. If travelling to foreign countries, your dog will need certain vaccinations and a health certificate, which normally need to be done four weeks before departure. You must also be sure that you've made all the arrangements necessary to bring your dog back home to the UK, without it needing to go into quarantine under the rabies regulations. Your vet can give you the most recent information. If your trip is to southern Europe, ask for a treatment against ticks (you can read more about this in the 'Parasites' chapter).

Be careful if you're planning to go to southern Europe. There are certain mosquito species that can transmit the larvae of the heartworm. Dogs become infected by mosquito bites. The larvae can grow into worms more than 20 cm (8 in) long. These parasites remain in the heart or in the pulmonary artery. Grown worms can cause serious health problems. When fighting heartworms, remains of the worms can cause problems in the blood vessels. Ask your vet about a safe treatment against heartworms if your travel destination is in southern Europe.

Travelling with your Staffordshire Bull Terrier

Although you might like the idea of taking your dog on holidays with you, you need to ask yourself honestly if your pet enjoys it as much. Staffords won't enjoy travelling to a hot country, as they don't cope well with heat. Travelling in the car for days is also not normally their preference. Some dogs badly suffer from carsickness. There are good treatments available, but you need to ask yourself whether you are really doing your dog a favour with them.

If you do decide to take your dog with you, make regular stops at safe places during your journey, as your dog needs to have a good run once in a while. Take plenty of fresh drinking water with you, as well as enough of the food your dog is used to. Don't leave your dog in the car standing in the sun. It can quickly be overcome by the heat, which can have fatal consequences. If you really cannot avoid it, park the car in the shade as far as possible and open a window a bit for fresh air. Even if you have taken these precautions: Never stay away long!

Always bear in mind that Staffords generally do not cope well with heat. Due to their coat, they can easily become overheated. Adapt the amount of exercise to the weather. Don't go for hour-long walks during the day, don't let your dog run beside the bike and don't let it chase after balls or sticks. On hot summer days, try to go for walks early in the morning or later in the evening. During the day, limit walks to a small stroll round the block. Also don't take your Staffordshire Bull Terrier to the beach on hot days. Although there is water available, there is still a big risk of your dog suffering a heatstroke.

If you are travelling by plane or ship, you need to inform yourself well in advance whether your dog is allowed to go with you and what rules apply. Allow plenty of time for your preparations, so that you can find an alternative if necessary.

Maybe you decide not to take your dog with you, and you then need to find somewhere for it to stay. Arrangements for a place in kennels need to be made well in advance. Certain vaccinations will be required, which need to be given a minimum of one month before the stay.

If your dog can't be accommodated in the homes of relatives or friends, it might be possible to have an acquaintance stay in your house. This also needs to be arranged well in advance, as it may be difficult to find someone who can do this. Always ensure that your dog can be traced should it run away or get lost while on holiday. A little tube with your address, or a tag with home and holiday addresses, can avoid a lot of problems.

Moving home

Dogs generally become more attached to humans than to the house they live in. Moving home is usually not a problem for them. But it can be useful to let your dog get to know its new home and the area around it before moving.

If you can, leave your Stafford somewhere else (with relatives, friends, or in kennels) on the day of the move. The chance of it running away or getting lost is then practically non-existent. Once you have completed your move, you can pick your dog up and let

it quietly get familiar with its new environment. Give it its own place in the house at once and it will quickly adapt. At the beginning, always walk your dog on a lead, because an animal can get lost in new surroundings too. Always take a different route so that it gets to know the neighbourhood well.

Don't forget to get your new address and phone number engraved on your dog's tag. Send a change of address notice to the institution that has any chip data. Dogs must sometimes be registered in a new community (just as people), and you will be sent a bill for a dog licence. In many communities, you get part of your licence fee back if you move within the year you paid for.

Feeding your Staffordshire Bull Terrier

A dog is actually more of an omnivore than a carnivore. In the wild it would eat its prey complete with skin and fur, including the bones, stomach, and the innards with their semi-digested vegetable material.

In this way the dog supplements its meat menu with the vitamins and minerals it needs. This is also the basis for feeding a domestic dog.

Ready-made foods

It's not easy for a layman to put together a complete menu for a dog, including all the necessary proteins, fats, vitamins and minerals in just the right proportions and quantities. Meat alone is certainly not a complete meal for a dog, as it contains too little calcium. A continuous calcium deficiency will lead to bone defects, and particularly for a fast-growing puppy this can cause serious skeletal deformities. If you put its food together yourself, you can easily give your dog too much in terms of vitamins and minerals, which can also be bad for your dog's health.

You can avoid these problems by giving your Stafford ready-made food of a good brand. These products are well balanced and contain everything your dog needs. Supplements, such as vitamin preparations, are superfluous. The amount of food your dog needs depends on its weight and activity level. You can find guidelines on the packaging.

Split the food into two meals per day if possible, and ensure that there's always a bowl of fresh drinking water next to its food. Give your Stafford the time to digest its food and don't let it outdoors straight after a meal. A dog should also never play on a full stomach. This can cause stomach torsion (the stomach turning over), which can be fatal for your dog.

Because the nutritional needs of a Stafford depend, among other things, on its age and way of life, there are many different types of dog food available. There are "light" foods for less active dogs, "energy" foods for working dogs and gundogs and "senior" foods for older dogs.

Canned foods, mixers and dry foods

Ready-made foods, which are available at pet shops or in the supermarket, can roughly be split into canned food, mixer and dry food. Whichever form you choose, ensure that it's a complete food with all the necessary nutrients. You can see this on the packaging.

Most dogs love canned food. Although the better brands are composed well, they do have one disadvantage: they are soft. A dog fed only on canned food will sooner or later have problems with its teeth (plaque, paradontosis).

Besides canned food, give your Stafford dry foods or dog chews at certain times.

Mixer is a food consisting of chunks, dried vegetables and grains. Almost all the moisture has been extracted. The advantages of mixer are that it is light and keeps well. You add a certain amount of warm water and the meal is ready. A disadvantage is that it must definitely not be fed without water. Without the extra fluid, mixer will absorb the fluids present in the stomach, which can cause serious problems. Should your dog manage to get at the bag and enjoy its contents, you must immediately give it plenty to drink.

Dry foods also have had moisture extracted, but not as much as mixer. The advantage of dry foods is that they are hard, forcing the dog to use its jaws. During chewing tartar is removed and the gums are massaged.

Dog chew products

Naturally, once in a while you want to spoil your dog with something extra. Don't give it pieces of cheese or sausage as these contain too much salt and fat. There are various products available at pet shops that a dog will find delicious and which are also healthy, especially for its teeth. You'll find a large range of varying quality in the pet shop.

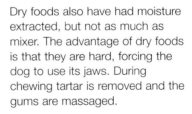

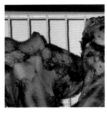

Smoked bones

Cowhide chews

The butcher's left-overs

The bones of slaughtered animals have traditionally been given to the dog, and dogs are crazy about them, but they are not without risks. Pork and poultry bones are too weak for a Staffordshire Bull Terrier's strong jaws. They can splinter and cause serious injury to the intestines. Beef bones are more suitable, but they must first be cooked to kill off dangerous bacteria. Pet shops carry a range of smoked, cooked and dried abattoir residue, such as pigs' ears, bull penis, tripe sticks, oxtails, gullet, dried muscle meat and hoof chews.

Fresh meat

If you do want to give your dog fresh meat occasionally, never give it raw, but always boiled or roasted. Raw (or not fully cooked) pork or chicken can contain life-threatening bacteria. Chicken can be contaminated by the notorious salmonella bacteria, while pork can carry the Aujeszky virus. This disease is incurable and will quickly lead to your pet's death.

Cowhide and buffalo hide chews

Dog chews are usually made of buffalo hide or cowhide. The hide is pressed or knotted into chews. Your dog can enjoy chews in the form of little shoes, twisted sticks, lollies, balls and various other shapes. Nice to look at and a nice change. Never buy chews that are too small, as they can easily go down the wrong way if the dog becomes greedy. Throw away small left-over bits of dog chews.

Munchie sticks

Munchie sticks are green, yellow, red or brown coloured sticks of various thicknesses. They consist of ground buffalo hide with a number of often undefined additives. Dogs usually love them because these sticks have been dipped in the blood of slaughtered animals. The composition and quality of these between-meal treats is not always clear. Some are fine, but there have also been sticks found that contained high levels of cardboard and even paint

residues. Choose a product whose ingredients are clearly labelled.

Overweight?

Recent investigations have shown that many dogs are overweight. A dog usually becomes too fat because of over-feeding and lack of exercise. Use of medicines or a disease is rarely the cause.

Dogs that become too fat are often given too much food or too many treats between meals. Gluttony or boredom can also be a cause, and a dog often puts on weight following castration or sterilisation. Due to changes in hormone levels it becomes less active and consumes less energy. Finally, simply too little exercise alone can lead to a dog becoming overweight.

You can use the following rule of thumb to check whether your dog is overweight: you should be able to feel its ribs, but not see them. If you can't feel its ribs then your dog is much too fat. Overweight dogs live a passive life; they play and run too little and tire quickly. They also suffer from all kinds of medical problems (problems in joints and heart conditions). They usually die younger too.

So it's important to make sure that your dog doesn't become too fat. Always follow the guidelines on food packaging. Adapt them if

your dog is less active or gets lots of snacks. Try to ensure that your dog gets plenty of exercise by playing and running with it as much as you can. If your dog starts to show signs of putting on weight, you can switch to a low-calorie food. If it's really too fat and reducing its food quantity doesn't help, then a special diet is the only solution.

**Good (daily) care is
extremely important for
your dog. A well cared-for
dog is less likely to
become ill.**

Caring for your dog is not only
necessary but also a pleasure, as
master and dog give each other all
their attention for a moment. It is
also a good opportunity for
playing and cuddling.

The coat

Good coat care involves regularly
brushing or combing the coat and
checking for parasites. How often
a dog needs to be brushed or
combed depends on the length of
the coat. The Stafford has a short,
smooth coat and therefore does
not need to be brushed very
often. It is, however, advisable to
brush it on a regular basis,

especially during moulting, so
that all loose hair is removed from
the coat. Be aware that your
Stafford will lose hair throughout
the year and that you will find it
all over the house. It is thus
preferable to brush your dog
outdoors, as you will then have
less trouble with dog hair flying all
over the house.

Always use the right tools when
caring for your dog's coat. Combs
must not be too sharp. Choose a
brush made of rubber or natural
hair. Always brush from head to
tail, following the direction the hair
lays in. If you get your Stafford
used to having its coat cared for
from a young age, it will quickly
learn to enjoy its grooming
sessions. Regularly check your
dog for fleas and ticks (also see
chapter 'Parasites').

Only bathe your Staffordshire Bull Terrier when it is absolutely necessary, and always use a special dog shampoo when doing so. Make sure that no shampoo can get into your dog's ears and eyes, and always rinse the suds out well. Only let your dog out when it is completely dry, as dogs can catch colds too! Your vet can prescribe certain medicinal shampoos for different skin conditions. Always follow the instructions. Good flea control is very important to prevent skin and coat disorders.

You need to fight fleas not only on the dog itself, but also in its environment. Coat problems can also be the result of allergies to certain feed components. In this case, the vet can prescribe a hypoallergenic diet.

Teeth

Your Stafford needs to be able to eat properly to stay in good condition. It thus needs healthy teeth. Therefore check your dog's teeth regularly. If you think that all is not well, contact your vet. Regular feeds of hard dry food help to keep your dog's teeth clean and healthy. There are special dog chews that help to prevent build-up of tartar and to keep the breath fresh.

The best way to keep your dog's teeth healthy is by brushing them regularly. You can use a special

toothbrush for dogs for this, but a piece of gauze wrapped round a finger will also do the job. If you get your dog used to having its teeth cleaned at a young age, you won't have any problems later. You can also get an older dog used to having its teeth cared for. With a dog treat as a reward, it certainly won't mind.

Nails

On a Stafford with healthy round feet that regularly walks on hard surfaces, the nails will grind themselves down to the right length. It is not necessary to clip them in this case. It won't do any harm, however, to check the length of its nails at certain times, especially on dogs that don't go out on the streets a lot or that only walk on soft ground. Also remember to check the fifth nail on the inside of the front paws. This nail does not wear off, as it does not touch the ground. With the help of a piece of paper, you can easily see if your dog's nails are too long. If you can push the paper between the ground and the nail of the (standing) dog, the nail has the right length.

Nails that are too long can bother a dog. It can injure itself when scratching. They thus need to be cut back. You can do this with special scissors, which you can buy in the pet shop. Be careful not to cut the nail too far back, as you might cut into the quick. This can bleed profusely. If you feel unsure about cutting your dog's nails, let the vet or a grooming parlour do this necessary task.

Eyes

You need to clean your dog's eyes every day, as 'sleepies' and bits of dried tear fluid can collect in the corners of the eyes. You can easily remove these by wiping downwards with your thumb. If you do not like doing this, you can use a bit of toilet paper or a tissue.

Cleaning your dog's eyes only takes a few seconds a day, so don't miss it! If the sleepies become yellow and slimy, it is usually a sign of a serious irritation or an infection. Eye drops (available from your vet's) usually solve this problem quite quickly. Conditions of the third eyelid need to be corrected surgically.

Ears

The ears are often forgotten when caring for dogs, but they must be checked at least once a week. If your dog's ears are very dirty or have too much wax, you must clean them. This should preferably be done with a clean cotton cloth, which is moistened with some warm water or babyoil. It is inadvisable to use cotton wool due to the fluff it can leave behind. Never enter the ear canal with an object. If your Stafford is constantly shaking its head or scratching at its ears, you need to check them for ear mites. Your vet can prescribe a treatment to kill off the mites.

It is very important that your Stafford is well brought up and that it listens to you. This will make it not only more pleasant for you, but also for your environment.

A puppy can learn what it may and may not do in a playful manner. Rewarding and consistency are very important aids when bringing up your dog. If you always reward it for good behaviour with your voice, a pat or a treat, it will quickly learn to obey. A puppy course can help you along the way.

The life expectancy of a Staffordshire Bull Terrier is twelve to fourteen years. They mature quite late, but they also stay young, both physically and mentally, quite long. A good upbringing is thus very important for your puppy.

The Staffordshire Bull Terrier is a very sporty dog, which enjoys walking and running next to the bike, and it has great stamina.

(Dis)obedience

A dog that won't obey you is not just a problem for you, but also for your surroundings. It's therefore important to avoid unwanted behaviour. In fact, this is what training your dog is all about, so get started early. 'Start 'em young!' should be your motto.

An untrained dog is not just a nuisance, but can also cause dangerous situations by running into the road, chasing joggers or jumping at people. A dog must be trained out of this undesirable behaviour as quickly as possible.

The longer you let it go on, the more difficult it will become to correct. The best thing to do is to attend a special obedience course. This won't only help to correct the dog's behaviour, but its owner also learns how to handle undesirable behaviour at home. A dog must not only obey its master during training, but at home too.

Always be consistent when training good behaviour and correcting annoying behaviour. This means your dog may always behave in a certain way, or must never behave that way. Think

about whether you will find a puppy's behaviour, such as snapping at hands and jumping at people, acceptable with an adult dog. Always reward your dog for good behaviour and never punish it after the event for any wrongdoing. If your dog finally comes after you've been calling it a long time, then reward it. If you're angry because you had to wait so long, it may feel it's actually being punished for coming. It will probably not obey at all next time for fear of punishment.

Try to take no notice of undesirable behaviour, as your dog will perceive your reaction (even a negative one) as a reward for this behaviour. If you need to correct your dog, then do it immediately. Use your voice or grip it by the scruff of its neck and push it to the ground. This is the way a bitch calls her pups to order. Rewards for good behaviour are, by far, preferable to punishment; they always achieve a better result.

When bringing up your Staffordshire Bull Terrier, bear in mind that, despite their appearance, they are very good-natured, friendly dogs. They

cannot cope with too much pressure. If you put your dog under too much pressure when bringing it up, it will result in undesirable behaviour. It is much better for your Staffordshire Bull Terrier if you bring it up in a playful manner. Your dog is very sensitive to your voice and thus not difficult to teach. Staffordshire Bull Terriers are also very intelligent and enjoy working for their master.

House-training

The very first training (and one of the most important) that a dog needs is house-training. The basis for good house-training is keeping a close eye on your puppy. If you pay attention, you will notice that it will sniff around a long time and turn around a certain spot before doing its business there. Pick it up gently and place it outdoors, always at the same place. Reward it abundantly if it does its business there.

Another good moment for house-training is after eating or sleeping. A puppy often needs to do its business at these times. Let it relieve itself before playing with it, otherwise it will forget to do so and you'll not reach your goal. For the first few days, take your puppy out for a walk just after it's eaten or woken up. It will quickly understand your intention, especially if it's rewarded with a dog biscuit for a successful attempt.

Of course, it's not always possible to go out after every snack or snooze. Lay newspapers at different spots in the house. Whenever the pup needs to do its business, place it on a newspaper. After some time it will start to look for a place itself. Then start to reduce the number of newspapers. Finally, there will be just one newspaper left, at the front or back door. The puppy will learn to go to the door if it needs to relieve itself. Then you put it on the lead and go out with it. You can eventually remove the last newspaper. Your puppy is now house-trained.

One thing that certainly won't work is punishing an accident after the event. A dog whose nose is rubbed in its urine or its droppings won't understand that at all. It will only get frightened of you. Here too, rewarding works much better than punishment. An indoor kennel or cage can be a good tool to help in house-training. A puppy won't foul its own nest, so a kennel can be a good solution for the night, or during periods in the day when you can't watch it. But an indoor kennel must not become a prison where your dog is locked up day and night.

First exercises

The basic commands for an obedient dog are those for sit, lie down, come and stay. You can teach a pup to sit by holding a piece of dog biscuit above its nose and then slowly moving it backwards. The puppy's head will also move backwards until its hind legs slowly go down. At that moment you call 'Sit!'. After a few attempts, it will quickly remember this nice game. Use the 'Sit!' command before you give your dog its food, put it on the lead, or before it's allowed to cross the street.

Teaching the command to lie down is similar. Instead of moving the piece of dog biscuit backwards, move it down vertically until your hand reaches the ground and then forwards. The dog will also move its forepaws forwards and lie down on its own. At that moment call 'Lie down!' or 'Lay!'. This command is useful when you want your Stafford to be quiet.

Two people are needed for the 'Come!' command. One holds the dog back while the other runs away. After about fifteen metres (50 ft), he stops and enthusiastically calls 'Come!'. The other person now lets the dog go, and it should obey the command at once. Again you reward it abundantly. The 'Come!' command is useful in many situations and good for safety too.

A dog learns to stay from the sitting or lying position. While it's

sitting or lying down, you call the command 'Stay!' and then step back one step. If the dog moves with you, quietly put it back in position, without displaying anger. If you do react angrily, you're actually punishing it for coming to you, and you'll only confuse your dog. It can't understand that coming is rewarded one time, and punished another. Once the dog stays nicely, reward it abundantly. Practise this exercise while increasing the distances between your dog and yourself (at first no

more than one metre/ 3 ft). The 'Stay!' command is useful when getting out of the car.

Obedience courses

Obedience courses to help you bring up your dog are available throughout the UK. These courses do not just teach owner and dog a lot, but are also fun. Make sure that you ask about the method of training in advance. Look for a dog school where the emphasis is on rewarding good behaviour. If the dogs are rewarded too little, your Stafford will soon lose its interest and fun in training. Teaching good behaviour has to be done in a playful manner.

With a puppy, you can begin with a puppy training course. This is designed to provide the basic training. A puppy that has attended such a course has learned about all kinds of things that will confront it in later life: other dogs, humans, traffic and more. The puppy will also learn obedience and to follow a number of basic commands. Apart from all that, attention will be given to important subjects such as grooming, being alone, travelling in a car, and doing its business in the right places.

The next step after a puppy course is a course for young dogs. This course repeats the basic exercises and ensures that the growing dog doesn't get into bad habits. After this, the dog can move on to an obedience course for fully grown dogs.

For more information on where to find courses in your area, contact your local kennel club. You can get its address from the Kennel Club of Great Britain in London. In some areas, the RSPCA organises obedience classes and your local branch may be able to give you information.

Play and toys

There are various ways to play with your Stafford. You can romp and run with it, but also play a number of games, such as retrieving, tug-of-war, hide-and-seek and catch. A tennis ball is ideal for retrieving, and you can play tug-of-war with an old sock or a special tugging rope. Start with tug-of-war only when your dog is a year old. A puppy must first get its second teeth and then they need several months to strengthen. There's a real chance of your dog's teeth becoming deformed if it starts playing tug-of-war too soon. You can use almost anything for a game of hide-and-seek. Frisbees are ideal for catching games. Never use too small a ball for games, as it can easily get lodged into the dog's throat.

Play is extremely important. Not only does it strengthen the bond between dog and master, but it's

also healthy for both. Make sure that you're always the one that ends the game. Only stop when the dog has brought back the ball or frisbee, and make sure that you always win the last tug-of-war. This confirms your dominant position in the hierarchy. Use these toys only during play, so that the dog doesn't forget their significance.

When choosing a special dog toy, remember that dogs are hardly careful with them. So always buy toys of good quality, which a Stafford can't easily destroy. Be also very careful with sticks and twigs. The latter, particularly, can easily splinter. A splinter of wood in your dog's throat or intestines can cause awful problems. Throwing sticks or twigs can also be dangerous. If they stick into the ground, a dog can easily run into them with its mouth open.

If you want to do more than just playing the odd game with your dog, you can do lots of different types of dog sports. If you are looking for a challenge, have a look at different activities such as flyball, dogfrisbee, agility and obedience certificates (see chapter 'Sports and shows').

Aggression

Staffordshire Bull Terriers are normally never aggressive towards humans. They were used as fighting dogs in the past, but they were never trained to attack people. This is why they are also no good as farm dogs or guard dogs. It can, however, happen that your Stafford is less friendly towards other animals or people. It is therefore good to have some background information about aggression in dogs. There are two different main types of aggressive behaviour in dogs: The anxious-aggressive dog and the dominant-aggressive dog.

An anxious-aggressive dog can be recognised by its pulled-back ears and its lowly held tail. It will have pulled in its lips, baring all teeth including the molars. This dog is aggressive because it's very frightened and feels cornered. It would prefer to run away, but if it can't then it will bite to defend itself. It will grab its victim anywhere it can. The attack is usually brief and as soon as the dog can see a way to escape it's gone. In a confrontation with other dogs it will normally turn out as the loser. It can become even more aggressive once it's realised that people or other animals are afraid of it. You can't change this behaviour just like that. You first have to try to understand what the dog is afraid of. Getting professional help is a good idea here, as the wrong approach can easily make the problem worse.

The dominant-aggressive dog's body language is very different. Its ears are pricked and its tail is raised and stiff. This dog will go only for its victim's arms, legs or throat. It is self-assured and highly placed in the dog hierarchy. Its attack is a display of power rather than a consequence of fear. This dog needs to know who's the boss. You must bring it up rigorously and with a strong hand. An obedience course can help.

A dog may also show aggression when in pain. This is a natural defensive reaction. In this case try to resolve the dog's fear as far as possible. Reward it for letting you get to the painful spot. Be careful, because a frightened dog in pain may also bite its master! Muzzling it can help prevent problems if you have to do something that may be painful. Never punish a dog for this type of aggression!

Fear

If your dog behaves in a frightened manner, the reason can usually be found in the first few weeks of its life. A lack of new experiences in this very important so-called 'socialisation phase' has a big influence on the adult dog's behaviour. If a dog does not get to see humans, other dogs or other animals during this phase, it will be afraid of them later. This is common with dogs that have grown up in a barn or kennel with basically no human contact. As mentioned earlier, fear can lead to aggression. It is thus very important that your dog gets as many new experiences as possible during its first few weeks. Take it into town in the car or on the bus, walk down a busy street with it and let it have lots of contact with people, other dogs and other animals/ pets.

It's a huge task to turn an anxious, poorly socialised dog into a real pet. It will probably take an enormous amount of attention, love, patience and energy to get such an animal used to everything around it. Reward it often and give it plenty of time to adapt and, over time, it will learn to trust you and become less anxious. Try not to force anything, because that will always have the reverse effect. Here too, an obedience course can help a lot.

A dog can be especially afraid of strangers. Have visitors give it

something tasty as a treat when they arrive. Put a can of dog biscuits by the door, so that your visitors can spoil your dog when they come in the door. Once again, don't try to force anything. If the dog is still frightened, it is best to leave it in peace.

Dogs are often frightened in certain situations; well-known examples are thunderstorms and fireworks. In these cases try to ignore your dog's anxious behaviour. If you react to its whimpering and whining, it's the same as rewarding it. If you ignore its fear completely, your dog will quickly learn that nothing is wrong. You can speed up this 'learning process' by rewarding its positive behaviour.

Rewarding

Rewarding forms the basis for bringing up a dog. Rewarding good behaviour works far better than punishing bad behaviour and rewarding is also much more fun. Over time the opinions on how to bring up dogs have gradually changed. In the past, a sharp pull on the lead was considered the appropriate way to correct bad behaviour. Today, experts view rewards as a positive incentive to get dogs to do what we expect of them.

There are many ways of rewarding your Stafford. The usual ways are a pat or a friendly word, even

without a tasty treat to go with it. When bringing up a puppy, a tasty treat at the right moment will do wonders, though. Make sure that you always have something tasty in your pocket to reward it for good behaviour.

Another form of reward is play. Dogs love to play. Whenever your dog notices that you have a ball in your pocket, it won't go far from your side. As soon as you've finished playing, put the ball away. This way your dog will always do its best in exchange for a game. Despite the emphasis you put on rewarding good behaviour, a dog can sometimes be a nuisance or disobedient. You must correct such behaviour immediately. Always be consistent: once 'no' must always be 'no'.

Barking

Dogs that bark too much and too often are a nuisance for their surroundings. A dog-owner may tolerate barking up to a point, but neighbours are often annoyed by the unnecessary noise. Luckily, Staffordshire Bull Terriers do not bark excessively by nature. It might still happen, however, that your puppy imitates and adopts the yapping of other dogs in the area. Don't encourage your puppy to bark and yelp in that case. Of course, it should be able to announce its presence, but if it goes on barking it must be called to order with a strict 'Quiet!'. If the

puppy does not obey, you can hold its muzzle closed with your hand for a moment.

A dog will sometimes bark for long periods when left alone. It feels threatened and tries to get someone's attention by barking. If a dog has been (sub)consciously rewarded for barking, it can carry on with this behaviour for some time. There are special training programmes for this problem, where a dog learns that being alone is nothing to be afraid of, and that its master will always return.

This is how you can practise with your dog: Leave the room and come back in at once. Reward your dog if it stays quiet. Gradually increase the length of your absences and keep rewarding it as long as it remains quiet. Never punish your dog if it does bark or yelp. It will never understand punishment afterwards, and this will only make the problem worse. Never go back into the room as long as your dog displays the unwanted behaviour, as it will view this as a reward.

You might want to make your dog feel more comfortable by switching the radio on for company during your absence. It will eventually learn that you always come back and the barking will reduce. If you don't get the required result, attend an obedience course with your dog.

Dogs, and thus also Staffordshire Bull Terriers, follow their instincts, and reproduction is one of nature's most important processes. This is of benefit to people who enjoy breeding dogs.

Those who simply want a 'cosy companion' however, will miss the regular adventures with females on heat and unrestrainable males like a hole in the head. But knowing a little about the reproduction of dogs will help you to understand why they behave the way they do, and what measures you need to take when this happens.

Liability

There is much more connected to breeding dogs than simply 1+1= many. If you're planning to breed with your Staffordshire Bull Terrier, be on your guard. The whole affair can quite easily turn into a financial disaster, because, under the law, a breeder is liable for the 'quality' of his puppies. It is also advisable to ensure that both animals have full papers. Be therefore meticulous in your search for a mating partner for your dog.

The breed association places high demands on animals used for breeding. They need to be checked for possible (hereditary) abnormalities. By applying to these rules, a breeder shows that he cares. If you breed a litter and sell the puppies without these tests having been made, you can be held liable by the new owners for any possible costs resulting from any hereditary abnormality! And these (vet's) bills can be very expensive! It is therefore advisable to contact a breed association if you're thinking about breeding a litter.

The female in season

Staffordshire bitches become sexually mature at the age of six to twelve months. With this breed, there are a lot of bitches that have their first season when they are six to seven months old. This is quite young for dogs. A normal season lasts two to three weeks. During this time, the bitch loses drops of blood and is very appealing to males. The bitch is fertile during the second half of her season, and she will then accept dogs to mate. The best time for mating is between the ninth and thirteenth day of her season.

A female's first season is often shorter and less severe than those that follow. If you want to breed with your bitch, you must allow the first (and sometimes the second) season to pass. Most bitches go into season twice per year.

If you do plan to breed with your Staffordshire Bull Terrier bitch in the future, then sterilisation is not an option to prevent unwanted offspring. A temporary solution is a contraceptive injection, although this is controversial because of possible side effects such as womb infections.

Phantom pregnancy

A phantom pregnancy is a not uncommon occurrence with dogs. The female behaves as if she has a litter. She takes all kinds of things to her basket and treats them like puppies. Her milk teats swell up and sometimes milk is actually produced. The female will sometimes behave aggressively towards people or other animals, as if she is defending her young.

Phantom pregnancies usually begin two months after a season and can last a number of weeks. If it happens to a bitch once, it will often re-occur after every season. If she suffers under it a lot, sterilisation is the best solution, because constantly re-occuring phantom pregnancies increase the risk of womb or teat conditions.

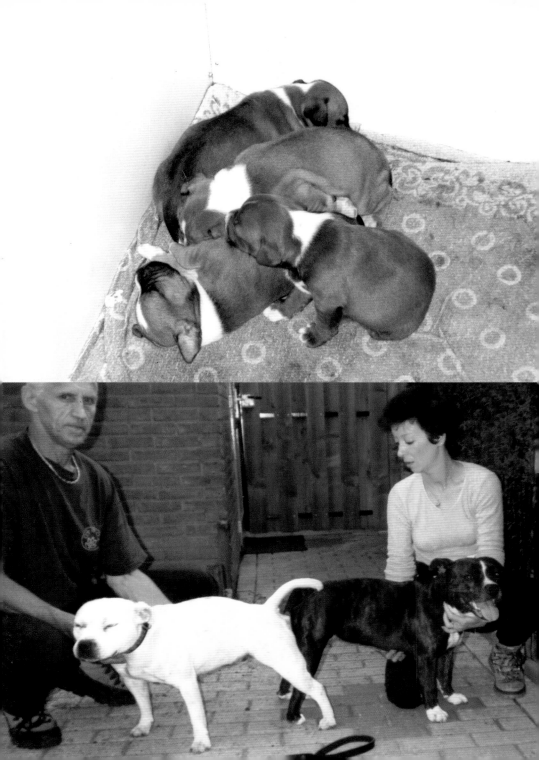

In the short term a hormone treatment is worth trying, perhaps also homeopathic medicines. Camphor spirit can give relief when teats are heavily swollen, but rubbing the teats with ice or a cold cloth (moisten and freeze) can also help relieve the pain. Feed the female less than usual, and make sure that she gets enough distraction and extra exercise.

Preparing to breed

If you do plan to breed a litter of puppies, you must first wait for your female to be physically and mentally fully grown before you have her covered. In any event you must wait until her second season. To mate a bitch, you need a male, preferably with a pedigree. In those countries where Staffords are classed as dangerous dogs, breeding animals are required to have full F.C.I. pedigrees. You could simply let your bitch out on the street and she would quickly return home pregnant. If you want to be serious about breeding, you should therefore keep a close eye on your bitch in season and never let her run free.

Think especially about the following: Accompanying a bitch through pregnancy, birth and the first eight to twelve weeks afterwards is a time-consuming affair. Never breed with Staffordshire Bull Terriers that have congenital defects, and this also applies to dogs with full papers. The same goes for hyperactive, nervous and shy dogs.

Contact one of the clubs on page 60 or 61 for more information on breeding and breeding regulations.

Pregnancy

It's often difficult to tell at first if a bitch is pregnant. Only after about four weeks can you feel the pups in her belly. She will now slowly become fatter and her behaviour will usually change. Her teats will swell during the last few weeks of pregnancy.

The average pregnancy lasts 63 days and costs the bitch a lot of energy. In the beginning she is fed her normal amount of food, but her nutritional needs increase in jumps during the second half of the pregnancy. Give her approximately fifteen percent more food each week from the fifth week on. The mother-to-be needs extra energy and proteins during this phase of her pregnancy. During the last weeks you can give her a concentrated food that is rich in energy, such as dry puppy food. Divide this into several small portions per day, as the bitch can no longer deal with large portions of food. Towards the end of the pregnancy, her energy needs can easily be one-and-a-half times more than usual. After about seven weeks the mother will start to demonstrate

After the mating the dogs are 'stuck'

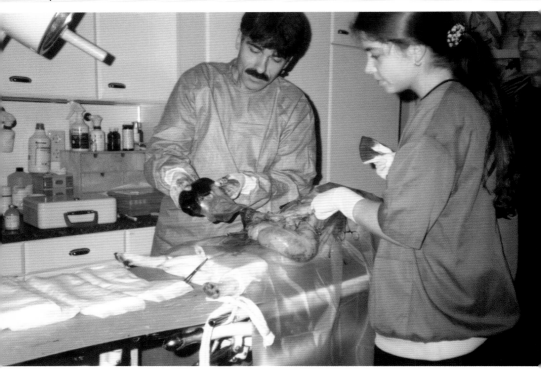

Birth by cesarian

nesting behaviour and to look for a place to give birth to her young. This might be her own basket or a special birthing box. This must be ready at least a week before the birth to give the mother-to-be time to get used to it. The basket or box should preferably be in a quiet place.

Birth

On average, three to nine puppies are born in a litter. The birth normally passes without problems. If you are in any doubt, you need to contact your vet immediately, of course!

Suckling and weaning

After giving birth, the mother starts to produce milk. The suckling period is very demanding. During the first three to four weeks the pups rely entirely on their mother's milk. During this time she needs extra food and fluids. This can be up to three to four times the normal amount. If she's producing too little milk, you can give both the mother and her young special puppy milk.

Here too, divide the high quantity of food the mother needs into several smaller portions. Again, choose a concentrated high-energy food and give her plenty of fresh drinking water. Do not give the bitch cow's milk, as this can cause diarrhoea.

You can give the puppies some supplemental solid food when they are three to four weeks old. There are special puppy foods available that follow on well from the mother's milk and that can easily be eaten with the puppies' milk teeth.

Ideally, the puppies are fully weaned at an age of six to seven weeks, i.e. they no longer drink their mother's milk. The mother's milk production gradually stops and her food needs also drop. Within a few weeks after weaning, the mother should be back to getting the same amount of food as before the pregnancy.

Castration and sterilisation

As soon as you are sure that your bitch should never bear a (new) litter, a vasectomy or sterilisation is the best solution. During sterilisation (in fact this is normal castration) the ovaries and often the uterus are removed surgically. The bitch no longer goes into season and can no longer become pregnant. The best age for a sterilisation is about eighteen months, when the bitch is more or less fully grown.

A male dog is usually only castrated for medical reasons or to correct undesirable sexual behaviour. During a castration the testicles are removed, which is a simple procedure and usually without complications. There is no special age for castration but, where possible, wait until the dog is fully grown. Vasectomy is sufficient where it's only a case of making the dog infertile. In this case the dog keeps its sexual drive but can no longer reproduce.

Staffordshire Bull Terriers love to be active. They enjoy doing things with their master. These dogs are also real allrounders.

If you regularly participate in activities with your Stafford, you will notice not only that the bond between both of you is becoming stronger, but also that your dog is a lot quieter in the house and a lot more obedient. Contact the breed association or dog schools in your area if you want more information on all the different sporting and showing opportunities.

Agility

Agility is a sport during which a dog has to master a certain course accompanied by its owner. The course consists of approximately twenty obstacles,

which need to be mastered faultlessly in a certain order without faults and as quickly as possible. The owner may direct the dog through the course with voice commands and gestures. The task is to overcome the obstacles as quickly as possible and with as few faults as possible. Agility competitions are organised by a lot of local kennel clubs.

Dogfrisbee

This is a sport that originated in America. The dog is required to catch a frisbee, which can be thrown in different ways. A special flexible dogfrisbee is used, which does not damage the dog's teeth. There are two different classes. The 'freestyle' class is accompanied by music. The thrower has 120 seconds to show as many throwing techniques as possible, and the dog has to catch the frisbee as often as possible. The other class is called 'minidistance'. Here, the thrower has only 60 seconds to throw the frisbee as far as possible. The further the frisbee flies, the more points the thrower receives.

Flyball

Flyball is another form of dog sports. A flyball team consists of dog owners, their dogs, a coach and a person loading the balls into the apparatus. The number of participants can vary from five to eight dog/ owner combinations. First the dog has to jump over four small hurdles, and then it has to push down a plank on the flyball apparatus with its paw. This action 'launches' a ball, which the dog needs to catch. The dog has to jump over the hurdles again on its way back and carry the ball to its owner as quickly as possible. The combination with the fastest time wins here too.

Behaviour and obedience

You can choose from a wide variety of obedience training courses, starting with puppy courses. Staffords normally really enjoy this type of training: as they are very focused on their master, they will happily try to carry out the exercises as well as possible. After the basic obedience training courses, you can carry on training for obedience diplomas.

Dog shows

Visiting a dog show is a pleasant experience for both dog and master, and for some dog-lovers it has become an intensive hobby. They visit countless shows every year. Others find it nice to visit an exemption show with their dog just once. It's worth making the effort to visit an exemption show where a judge's experienced eyes will inspect your Staffordshire Bull Terrier and assess it for build, paces, condition and behaviour. The judge's report will teach you your dog's weak and strong points. This can be very useful when choosing a mate for breeding, for example. You can also exchange experiences with other Stafford owners. Official dog shows are only open to dogs with pedigrees.

Ring training

If you've never been to an exemption show, you're probably tapping in the dark in terms of what will be expected of you and your dog. Many kennel clubs organise so-called ring training courses for dogs going to an exemption show for the first time. This training teaches you exactly what the judge will be looking for, and you can practise the correct techniques together with your dog.

Club matches

Almost all kennel clubs and breed associations organise club matches. You have to enter your dog in a certain class before the big day. These meetings are usually small and friendly and are often the first acquaintance dog and master make with a judge. This is an overwhelming experience for your dog - a lot of its contemporaries and a strange man or woman who fiddles around with it and peers into its mouth. After a few times, your dog will know exactly what's expected of it and will happily go to the next club match.

Championship shows

Various championship shows take place during the course of the year, all of which offer different prizes. These shows are much more strictly organised than club matches. Here, too, your dog must be registered in a certain class in advance and it will then be listed in a catalogue. On the day itself, the dog is kept in a cage (indoor kennel) until its turn comes up. During the judging in the ring, it's important that you show your dog at its best. The judge will give an official verdict and write a report. When all the dogs from that class have been judged, the winner is selected. You can pick up your report, and possibly your prize, after the class has finished.

The winners of the various classes will then compete for the title of Best of Breed. A winner will be chosen from the dogs belonging to the same breed group. The various winners of the different breed groups will then compete for Best in Show.

It goes without saying that your dog has to be in top condition for a show. The judge will not be pleased if your dog's coat is dirty and its paws are covered in mud.

Its nails must be clipped and the teeth free of tartar. The dog must also be free of any parasites or illnesses. A bitch must not be in season, and a dog should have both its testicles. Judges also don't like badly brought up, frightened or nervous dogs. If you want to know more about (exemption) shows, contact your local kennel club or the breed association.

Do not forget!

If you want to visit a show with your Staffordshire Bull Terrier, you need to be well prepared. You must certainly not forget the following:

For yourself:

- Registration card
- Food and drink
- Safety pin for the catalogue number
- Chair(s)

For your dog:

- Food and drink bowls and food
- Dog blanket and perhaps a cushion
- Show lead
- A brush
- Vaccination book and other papers for your dog

All dogs are vulnerable to various sorts of parasites. Parasites are tiny creatures that live at the expense of another animal. They feed on blood, skin and other body substances. There are two main types.

Internal parasites live within their host animal's body (tapeworm and roundworm) and external parasites live on the animal's exterior, usually in its coat (fleas and ticks), but also in its ears (ear mite).

Fleas

Fleas feed on a dog's blood. They cause not only itching and skin problems, but can also carry infections such as tapeworm. In large numbers they can even cause anaemia and dogs can also become allergic to a flea's saliva,

which can cause serious skin conditions.

So it's important that you treat your dog for fleas as effectively as possible. Do not just treat the animal itself, but also its surroundings. There are various medicines for treating your dog: drops for the neck and to put in its food, flea collars, long-life sprays and flea powders. There are various sprays in pet shops, which can be used to eradicate fleas in your dog's immediate surroundings. Choose a spray that kills both adult fleas and their larvae. If your dog goes in your car, you should spray that too.

Fleas can also affect other pets, so you should treat those too. When spraying a room, cover any aquarium or fishbowl present. If

Parasites

the spray reaches the water, it can be fatal for your fish! Your vet and pet shop have a wide range of flea treatments and can advise you further on the subject.

Ticks

Ticks are small, spider-like parasites. They feed on the blood of the animal or person they've settled on. A tick looks like a tiny, grey-coloured leather bag with eight feet. When it has sucked itself full, it is darker in colour and can easily be five to ten times its own size.

Dogs usually fall victim to ticks in bushes, woods or long grass. Ticks cause not only irritation by their blood-sucking, but can also carry a number of serious diseases. This applies especially to the Mediterranean countries, which can be infested with blood parasites. In our country these diseases are fortunately less common. But Lyme disease, which can also affect humans, has reached our shores. Your vet can prescribe a special treatment if you're planning to take your dog to southern Europe. It is important to fight ticks as effectively as possible. Check your dog regularly, especially when it's been running free in woods and bushes. It can also wear an anti-tick collar.

Removing a tick is simple using tick tweezers. Grip the tick with the tweezers, as close to the dog's skin as possible, and carefully pull it out. You can also grip the tick between your fingers and, with a turning movement, pull it carefully out. You must disinfect the spot where the tick was, using iodine to prevent infection. Never soak the tick in alcohol, ether or oil. In a shock reaction the tick may discharge the infected contents of its stomach into the dog's skin.

Worms

Dogs can suffer from various types of worm. The most common are tapeworm and roundworm. Tapeworm causes diarrhoea and poor condition. With a tapeworm infection you can sometimes find small pieces of the worm around the dog's anus or on its bed. In this case, the dog must be wormed immediately. You should also check your dog for fleas, as these can transmit the tapeworm infection.

Roundworm is another condition that reoccurs regularly. Puppies are often infected by their mother's milk. Roundworm causes problems (particularly in younger dogs), such as diarrhoea, loss of weight and stagnated growth. In serious cases the pup becomes thin, but with a swollen belly. It may vomit and you can then see the worms in its vomit. They are spaghetti-like tendrils. In its first year, a puppy regularly needs to be treated with a worm treatment. Adult dogs should be treated twice a year.

Tick

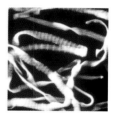

Tapeworm

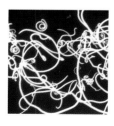

Roundworm

the **Staffordshire Bull Terrier**

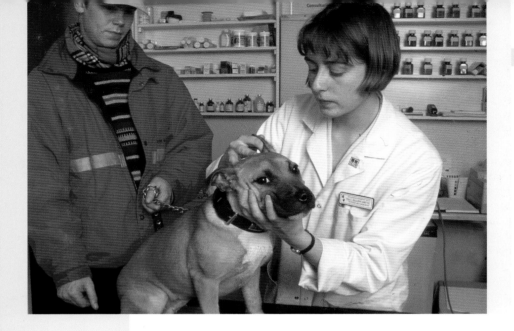

The Staffordshire Bull Terrier is a very healthy dog breed. No specific hereditary disorders are known of. Just as any other dog, however, your Stafford can become ill.

Anal Gland Disease

A dog that scoots over the ground with its bottom might be suffering from Anal Gland Disease (impacted anal glands). In this case you must empty the glands (or let the vet do it). You can feel the anal glands under the dog's tail, at the anus. If you think of a clock, these glands are positioned at around twenty to four. Your vet can teach you when and how to empty the anal glands (by squeezing them).

Corona

Corona is a virus disease that is accompanied by vomiting and diarrhoea. The symptoms are similar to those of a Parvo infection, but they are less severe. Apart from the symptoms mentioned under Parvo, Corona can also affect the mucous membranes. The symptoms for this are discharge from the eyes and nose. The disease is spread via excrements.

Rabies

This virus disease is fatal for humans and dogs alike. The virus is transmitted via saliva, and it enters the body via (small) wounds. Rabies spreads via the nerves all the way to the brain, which eventually causes the victim's death. After being bitten by an infected animal, it can take up to fifty days for the first symptoms to appear in the victim. The last phase of the illness is horrendous. At this point the virus has affected the brain, the dog is scared and crawls away into a corner, and its behaviour can turn into being wild and very aggressive. It will then destroy and attack anything in its surroundings. Luckily, Rabies does not exist in the UK (and quarantine laws are in place to keep it this way), but it can be found in continental Europe. If you plan to travel abroad with your dog, it needs to be vaccinated against Rabies. The disease is transmitted by saliva (bites) of foxes, badgers and other animals.

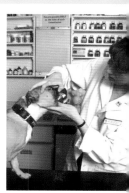

Canine Distemper

This illness, also known as Carré's Disease, is caused by a virus and is very infectious. The severity of the first symptoms, a runny nose and a little coughing, is often underestimated. Shortly after the

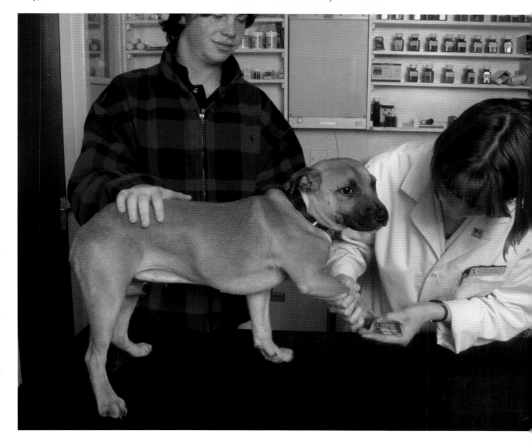

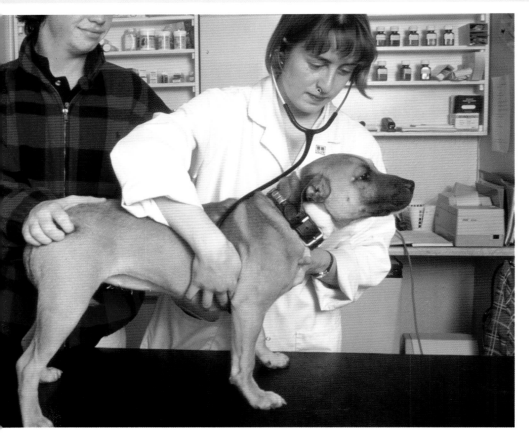

first symptoms, fever, lack of appetite, vomiting and/or diarrhoea follow. Inflammation of the throat, pus-like discharge from nose and eyes, twitching and cramps follow. A young dog may become critically ill. The virus causes inflammations in the intestines, but also Meningitis. A lot of dogs do not survive this disease. Of the dogs that do survive, many are left with permanent nerve damage, or at least a 'tic'. The dog will often display a behavioural disorder that it did not have before the illness, e.g. it finds it difficult to orientate itself or gets lost quickly. Canine Distemper is spread via saliva, urine and excrements.

Kennel Cough

The Kennel Cough Syndrome is an illness that is caused by various microorganisms, including Parainfluenza virus, Bordetella virus and others. Infection usually occurs where a lot of dogs are together, for example in a (boarding) kennel, at a show or on dog training grounds. This ailment of the respiratory system presents itself with a harsh scratchy cough, which is sometimes combined with damage to the lungs. Most of the time, the dogs aren't too ill, but they still need to be treated by a vet. The mucous membranes can be eased with cough medicine (thyme syrup) and taking your dog on a short break with lots of fresh air can do wonders. If you are leaving your dog in boarding kennels, it is advisable (and often mandatory) to vaccinate it as a precaution against this stubborn cough four weeks before you leave. Transmission is via the breath.

Parvo

Parvo is a highly contagious disease that is caused by a virus. A dog infected by the Parvovirus will often die. The virus is spread via the excrement of an infected dog. When healthy dogs sniff at this excrement, they become infected straight away. The virus spreads to the intestines, where it causes serious inflammation. Within a very short time, the dog will suffer from bloody diarrhoea, might vomit blood, will become drowsy, have a temperature and become critically ill. It will usually refuse to eat and drink and can thus become dehydrated. Most

dogs die of dehydration in combination with a severe loss of blood. Treatment therefore mainly consists of administering large amounts of fluids by infusion. Most dogs die within 48 hours after the first symptoms appear. In puppies, an infection can cause heart failure. Today, puppies are vaccinated against Parvo while still in the litter. Puppies that survive the illness might suddenly die later on in life due to Myocarditis, a heart condition that can be caused by Parvo.

Weil's Disease

Weil's Disease (Leptospirosis) is a disease caused by micro-organisms. The biggest chance of infection is in the spring and autumn. The disease can be fatal in younger dogs. Humans can also be infected by dogs and rats. A dog swimming in or drinking from contaminated water might be infected by bacteria via the mucous membranes and possibly small skin wounds. The bacteria establish themselves in the liver and kidneys. The symptoms are: high fever, doziness and muscle pain. The dog also lacks appetite, vomits and is very thirsty. It might also have nosebleed, dark urine and sometimes Yellow Fever. The disease is transmitted via the urine of infected dogs and rats.

Breed associations

Becoming a member of a breed club can be very useful for good advice and interesting activities. Contact the Kennel Club in case addresses or telephone numbers have changed.

Alyn & Deeside Staffordshire Bull Terrier Club
Sec. Mr A Moran
Tel No: 0161 320 6485

Downlands Staffordshire Bull Terrier Club
Sec. Mrs A Gatenby
Tel No: 01730 828402
www.downlands.org.uk

East Anglian Staffordshire Bull Terrier Club
Sec. Mrs L McFadyen
Tel No: 01992 427698
www.eastangliansbtclub.co.uk

East Midlands Staffordshire Bull Terrier Club
Sec. Mrs N Vann
Tel No: 01664 840570
www.emsbtc.co.uk

Merseyside Staffordshire Bull Terrier Club
Sec. Mr R Blackle.
Tel No:0151 287 6822
www.msbtc.co.uk

Morecambe Bay & Cumbria Staffordshire Bull Terrier Club
Sec. Mr G H Earle
Tel No: 01697 320217

North Eastern Staffordshire Bull Terrier Club
Sec. Miss J M E McLauchlan
Tel No: 01642 783948

North Of Scotland Staffordshire Bull Terrier Club
Sec. Ms J A Smith
Tel No: Not availble - for more information contact The Kennel Club

North West Staffordshire Bull Terrier Club
Sec. Miss S Houghton
Tel No: 01942 708161
www.northwestsbtclub.co.uk

Northern Counties Staffordshire Bull Terrier Club
Sec. Mrs C Lee
Tel No: 01423 863829

Northern Ireland Staffordshire Bull Terrier Club
Sec. Mr B Millen
Tel No: 02890 431580

Notts & Derby District Staffordshire Bull Terrier Club
Sec. Mrs.Jenny Smith
Tel No: 01332 781062

Potteries Staffordshire Bull Terrier Club
Sec.Mrs S A Reader.
Tel No: 01782 611514

Scottish Staffordshire Bull Terrier Club
Sec. Mr Fleming
Tel No: 0141 763 2349
www.ssbtc.co.uk

Southern Counties Staffordshire Bull Terrier Club
Sec. Mr Meneer
Tel No: For further information contact the Kennel Club
www.scsbts.freeserve.co.uk

Staffordshire Bull Terrier Club
Sec. Mr J Beaufoy
Tel No: 01299 403382
www.thesbtc.com

Staffordshire Bull Terrier Club Of South Wales
Sec. Mr J Holle
Tel No: 01792 542606
www.sbtcsw.co.uk

Western Staffordshire Bull Terrier Society
Sec. Mr Grimwood
Tel No: 01495 759254

The Kennel Club
1 Clarges Street
London, W1J 8AB UK
Tel: 0870 606 6750
Fax: 020 7518 1058
www.the-kennelclub.org.uk

Tips for the Staffordshire Bull Terrier

- Buy your Stafford puppy via the breed association and from a recognised breeder.
- If possible, visit several breeders before buying your puppy.
- Always ask to see the parent animals' pedigrees and declarations of health.
- Make a purchase contract before buying your puppy.
- Attend a puppy training course with your dog. It teaches both dog and master a lot.
- Its first journey is quite an adventure for a puppy. Make sure it's a nice one!
- Never buy a puppy whose mother you weren't able to see.
- Regularly feed your Stafford hard dry food and give it a dog chew. This will keep your dog's teeth healthy.
- Make sure that your dog doesn't become overweight.

Not too much food and plenty of exercise are the golden rules.
- Never leave a dog alone with small children.
- Do not let your puppy run endlessly after a ball or stick.
- Do not only treat fleas, but also their larvae.
- Organise a holiday stay or a dog sitter for your Stafford well in advance.

Group:	Terriers
Country of origin:	Great Britain
Original tasks:	Dog and badger fights, rat control
Present task:	Pet
Character:	Enthusiastic, friendly, attached to humans
Colours:	Brindle, red, fawn, white, black or blue, or one of these colours with white
Weight:	Dogs: 13-17 kg (28-38 lb)
	Bitches: 11 -15.4 kg (24-34 lb)
Height:	36 to 41 cm (14 -16 ins)
Life expectancy:	12 to 14 years

The Staffordshire Bull Terrier

the **Staffordshire Bull Terrier**